OUTDOOR EDUCATION LEARNING CE[NTER]
3830 Richmond Ave.
Houston, Texas 77027

PROJECTS WITH PLANTS
A Science at Work Book

PROJECTS WITH PLANTS
A Science at Work Book

BY SEYMOUR SIMON
illustrated by Lynn Sweat

FRANKLIN WATTS | NEW YORK | LONDON

Library of Congress Cataloging in Publication Data

Simon, Seymour.
    Projects with plants.

    (A Science at work book)
    SUMMARY: Includes short- and long-term projects designed to reveal basic facts about plants, their growth, and their nourishment.
    Bibliography: p.
    1. Botany–Experiments — Juvenile literature. [1. Botany–Experiments] I. Sweat, Lynn, illus. II. Title.
QK49.S56   581   73-5710
ISBN 0-531-02649-3

Text copyright © 1973 by Seymour Simon
Illustrations copyright © 1973 by Franklin Watts, Inc.
Printed in the United States of America
6 5 4

Also by the author

Science at Work: Easy Models You Can Make
Science at Work: Projects in Space Science
Science at Work: Projects in Oceanography

CONTENTS

Introduction 1

The Needs of Seeds 2

Seeds and Soil 4

Seed Planting Depth 6

Temperature and Seed Germination 8

Seeds Absorb Water 10

The Force of Growing Seedlings 12

Where Water Enters a Plant 14

Water Travels in Stems and Leaves 16

Photoperiodism 18

Sunlight and Plant Growth 22

Artificial Light and Plant Growth 24

Light Color and Plant Growth 26

Photosynthesis in Green Plants 28

Photosynthesis and Oxygen Production 30

The Growth of Bread Mold 32

The Growth of Bacteria 34

Plant Competition 36

Preventing Photosynthesis 38

Growing Plants Without Soil 40

Phototropism 42

Plants in a Maze 44

Geotropism 46

Seeds in Motion 48

Hydrotropism 50

Plant Growth Chemicals 52

Musical Plants 54

Plants That Eat Animals 56

For Further Reading 58

Where to Buy Supplies 59

Index 60

INTRODUCTION

Animals eat plants, but what kinds of plants eat animals? Can a plant grow its way through a maze? Do plants like music? How deep down in the ground should you plant a seed? Do seeds and plants need soil at all? You can find the answers to these and many other questions by carrying out the experiments and investigations in this book.

You don't need a garden, or a back yard, or a laboratory. You can do most of the projects at home, in a corner of your room, with simple, easily available materials. You can do most of the projects in winter as well as in summer.

There are a great variety of projects in the book. Some of them are simple and can be completed in a short time. Some projects are more difficult and will take a longer time to do. Perhaps you can start with some of the simple ones and then go on to try the long-term projects that interest you the most.

Try to work as a scientist does. Decide on a plan you will follow in your investigation. In many cases, you can easily vary the plans suggested in the book to fit your own interests. Keep a record of what you do and what you observe. Note the answers you find and the new questions that may arise as a result of your work.

The world of living plants is all around you, even in the air of your own room. You can use this book to help you explore that world.

THE NEEDS OF SEEDS

YOU WILL NEED: A package of lima bean seeds, three wide-mouthed glass jars, potting soil (a commercial preparation sold in gardening and variety stores), water, adhesive tape, a pencil, and a magnifying lens, if available.

WHAT TO DO: Clean and rinse the glass jars. Use the adhesive tape and a pencil to label and number each of the jars. Fill each jar about three-fourths full of potting soil. Don't pack the soil down too tightly. Plant five bean seeds in each jar. Poke each seed about one-half inch below the surface of the soil, spaced apart from the other seeds. Keep all three jars next to each other in a warm spot in your room.

Do not water jar number 1. Water jar number 2 just enough to keep the soil moist but not soggy. Water jar number 3 until water appears over the surface of the soil. Water jars 2 and 3 when needed so that they stay as described. Observe the jars each day for a week or two and keep a record of what you see.

WHAT TO LOOK FOR: The seeds in jar number 1 receive air but not water. The seeds in jar number 2 receive both water and air. The seeds in jar number 3 receive water, but because they are submerged, they do not receive any air.

What would you conclude if the seeds in jar number 2 are the only ones that germinate, that is, start to grow? After remaining in the dry soil for a week or two, will the seeds in jar number 1 germinate if you start adding a small amount of water? Does that ever happen out of doors in nature?

At the end of the experiment, examine the seeds in jar number 3. Have they changed in any way? Do they have an odor? What do you think has happened to them? Does an excessive amount of water, in actual conditions of nature, ever prevent any kinds of seeds from growing? Do you think that there might be other kinds of seeds that will grow underwater? How might you find out?

Take apart a dry seed and examine it closely. Use a magnifying lens if you have one available. Notice the waxy coat that covers and protects the seed. The two halves of the seed contain stored food. They are called cotyledons. Plants with seeds such as beans that have two cotyledons are called dicotyledons or dicots. Some seeds such as corn have a single cotyledon. They are called monocotyledons or monocots. Grasses are monocots. Between the cotyledons in a bean seed is the tiny plant called the embryo. The embryo plant grows to become the adult plant.

When you eat beans or other seeds, you are eating the food stored in the cotyledons. Think of all the different kinds of seeds that are used as food by man. You even eat grass seeds. Of course the grasses are wheat, rice, and oats, and the seeds are processed in different ways before they get to your table.

SEEDS AND SOIL

YOU WILL NEED: A package of lima bean seeds, three wide-mouthed glass jars, potting soil, aquarium gravel, cotton, a ruler, adhesive tape, and a pencil. Other kinds of planting materials: paper towels, vermiculite (available from a garden supply store), sand, or sawdust.

WHAT TO DO: Clean and rinse the glass jars. Number the jars, using adhesive tape and a pencil. Fill jar number 1 three-fourths full of potting soil, jar number 2 three-fourths full of gravel, and jar number 3 three-fourths full of cotton. Pack each material loosely. Plant five seeds about one-half inch below the surface of the material in each jar; the seeds should be spaced evenly away from each other. Plant the seeds close to the sides of the jars so that you can see them through the glass. Place the jars in a warm spot in your room. Water each jar the same amount, so that the soil and the cotton stay moist but not soggy. Each day record your observations on when and how many seeds germinate, how the seedlings look, and so on. Use the ruler to measure the height of any seedlings and record your findings.

WHAT TO LOOK FOR: Did seeds planted in all of the jars germinate? Was there any difference in the time it took for the seeds in the different jars to germinate? Did the seedlings grow at different rates?

Where do seedlings get the food they need to grow? Even if seedlings germinate in any moist material, do you think that they would continue to grow to full size equally well in all materials? How can you experiment to find out?

Try this same experiment with different kinds of planting materials, using other kinds of seeds. Follow the directions on the package for the seed depth in planting. Also try using other kinds of planting materials such as paper towels, vermiculite (a substance made from mica), sand, or sawdust. Do you notice any difference in the germination? What conclusions can you come to about whether soil is necessary for seeds to germinate?

SEED PLANTING DEPTH

YOU WILL NEED: Several wide-mouthed glass jars, packages of different seeds such as radish, bean, corn, and pea, potting soil, a ruler, adhesive tape, water, and a pencil.

WHAT TO DO: Clean and number each jar as in the previous experiments. Place a piece of adhesive tape on the side of each jar running from top to bottom. On the tape, rule lines at every inch starting from the top. Place soil in one of the jars until it reaches four inches from the top. Place five or six of one kind of seed on top of the soil close to the glass sides of the jar. Cover the seeds with two more inches of soil. Again place five or six seeds on the soil close to the glass. Cover these seeds with one and one-half inches of soil. Place another five or six seeds on the soil and cover them with one-half inch of soil. Do the same in each of the other jars, using a different kind of seed in each. You should have seeds planted at depths of one-half inch, two inches, and four inches.

Keep the jars in a warm spot in your room. Water them so that the soil stays moist but not soggy. Each day record how many and which seeds germinate in each jar. Also record how many seedlings come to the surface and from which depth. Keep records on what happens for a week to ten days.

WHAT TO LOOK FOR: How many seeds in each jar germinated at a depth of one-half inch? How many at two inches? How many at four inches? Was there any difference between different kinds of seeds? Was there any difference in the number that germinated at different depths? Does depth seem to have anything to do with how many seeds germinate?

How many seedlings appeared above the surface from the seeds planted at one-half inch? Did any seedlings come up from the seeds planted at two inches? Was there a difference in each of the different jars? Can you explain why fewer seedlings came to the surface from two inches than from one-half inch?

You have seen that seedlings get their food from the stored material in the cotyledon (see page 3). As they grow, green plants manufacture their own food when they are in sunlight. What would happen if a seed ran out of stored food in the cotyledon before it reached the surface and began to manufacture its own food? Does this help you to explain why few if any plants came up from the seeds planted at a depth of four inches? Why did some kinds of seeds planted at two inches come up to the surface while other kinds did not? Does the size of the seed make any difference in how deep it should be planted?

TEMPERATURE AND SEED GERMINATION

YOU WILL NEED: Packages of several different kinds of seeds such as radish, lettuce, and corn, three 6 x 6 inch pieces of cotton cloth for each kind of seed you use, rubber bands, water, a home refrigerator with a freezing compartment, and a pencil.

WHAT TO DO: Dip three of the cloths in water and wring them out. They should be moist but not dripping wet. Place twenty seeds of the same kind in each of the cloths, spacing the seeds evenly. Roll up the cloths and tie the ends with rubber bands. Label each with the kind of seed you are using. Place one of the rolls in the freezer section of your home refrigerator, the second roll in the refrigerator part, and the third roll in a warm spot in your room. Every day, for a week, unwrap each roll, count and record the number of seeds that have germinated. Moisten the rolls when needed. Follow the same procedure with different kinds of seeds.

WHAT TO LOOK FOR: How many seeds in each of the three groups germinated? Which ones germinated first? Did any kinds of seeds germinate in the freezer? Do you think that seeds can germinate when the temperature is below freezing out of doors? Can some kinds of seeds germinate at a lower temperature than other kinds? How can you find out?

Can the seeds kept in the freezer germinate if taken out and allowed to remain in warmer surroundings? What happens to the seeds kept in the refrigerator if you remove them to a warm place? Do seeds die if kept at too low a temperature for too long a period?

Some kinds of seeds benefit by staying at a low temperature before planting. Farmers found that planting certain kinds of seeds in the fall made them germinate sooner when spring came. Scientists then discovered that they could get the same effect by keeping seeds refrigerated for a number of days and then planting them. Apples, grains such as wheat and oats, pea seeds, and other farm crops can be treated in this way. The periods of time each kind of seed must be kept cold vary.

SEEDS ABSORB WATER

YOU WILL NEED: Two small glass jars with screw tops, a large package of bean seeds, water, a rubber band, and two strong plastic bags large enough to hold the jars.

WHAT TO DO: Fill up one glass jar with bean seeds. Add water until it covers the beans. Tightly screw on the lid of the jar. Place the jar in a plastic bag and seal the bag with a rubber band. Leave the bag containing the jar in a warm spot in your room for a day. Prepare another jar in the same way except do not add water to the second jar.

WHAT TO LOOK FOR: The process of water intake by seeds is called imbibition. Imbibition is the first step in germination. When a seed is put into water, it starts to take the water inside the seed coat. The tiny cells in the seed absorb the water. The seed swells up rapidly.

The swelling seeds expand and exert great pressure. The pressure is often enough to break a glass jar. Did your jar break in one day? Did anything happen to the seeds in the jar without water? What was the purpose of using a jar of seeds without water in this experiment?

You can do a similar experiment without breaking a jar if you like. Use two jars of the same size. Fill each with bean seeds to the halfway point. Rest a cardboard circle on top of the seeds in each jar. Place a piece of adhesive tape down the side of each jar and mark the position of the cardboard. Add enough water to one of the jars to wet the seeds.

Each hour observe the jars and mark on the tape the level of the cardboard. Was there any evidence of imbibition in the first hour? Does the rate of imbibition seem to stay about the same or does the water seem to be absorbed more quickly during the first hours? Did the cardboard on the dry seeds rise at all? What does this show?

THE FORCE OF GROWING SEEDLINGS

YOU WILL NEED: A package of lima bean seeds, plaster of Paris, water, and a coffee can.

WHAT TO DO: Soak five or six seeds in water for half a day. Place two cupsful of plaster of Paris in the coffee can. Add enough water to produce a mixture like heavy cream. Smooth off the top of the wet plaster. Push the seeds just below the surface to a depth of about one-quarter inch and cover with the plaster. Place the can in a warm spot in your room.

WHAT TO LOOK FOR: The plaster will become as hard as a rock in a day's time. Each day moisten the plaster. After a few days, the sprouting seeds will begin to push up the surface of the rock-like plaster. Do any of the seedlings break through? Can you see bulges in each of the places in which you planted the seeds?

Have you ever seen plants growing through roads or sidewalks? Often, plants will grow in the cracks of little-used buildings or roads. After a few years of disuse, roads or buildings become overgrown with plants breaking through the surface.

Sometimes the seeds of a large plant such as a tree are carried by animals or blown by the wind into a crack in a rock. The seeds sprout and begin to pry the crack further and further apart. As the seedling grows to become a tree, the rock may be split apart by the force of the growing roots and trunk.

Certain kinds of trees, such as willows, are usually not planted close to sidewalks. A willow tree's roots grow at a shallow depth below the ground and can cause a nearby sidewalk to buckle upward. Sometimes roots grow into pipes and sewers and break them apart with the force of their growth.

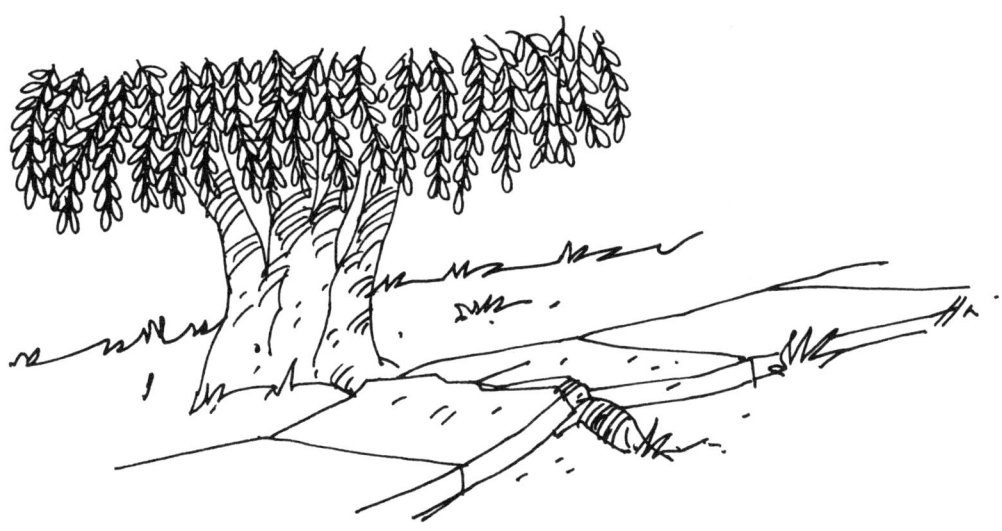

WHERE WATER ENTERS A PLANT

YOU WILL NEED: Two potted plants of the same kind, aluminum foil, water, and a watering can.

WHAT TO DO: You can grow plants from bean seeds or purchase small coleus or geranium plants. Don't water the plants for several days before you start the experiment. Use aluminum foil to cover the soil all around the stem of one of the plants. Hold the plant sideways over the sink and water the stem and leaves (but not the roots) of the plant. Try not to get any water into the soil. Now water the soil of the other plant. Place the plants in a warm spot in your room near a well-lighted window.

WHAT TO LOOK FOR: In a day or two, the plant in the aluminum-covered pot will begin to wilt and die. If you want to save it, you must water the soil. Do the stem or leaves of a plant take in water? How do you know? What part of a plant is in the soil? How does this experiment show that water enters a plant through the roots?

The roots of a plant have many tiny little structures called root hairs. Water enters a plant through these root hairs by a process called osmosis. You can observe the root hairs in the following way. Place a sheet of paper towel on the bottom of a pan or a shallow dish. Soak the paper with water and then pour off any excess. Place a number of small seeds on the wet paper and cover the dish with a piece of plastic wrapping paper.

Peel back the plastic wrapping paper each day to let some air in and to check that the paper towel stays moist. After several days you can examine the roots. Use a magnifying lens to find the fuzzy root hairs along the side of the root. Draw a picture of what you see. Read about root hairs in one of the books about plants listed in "For Further Reading" on page 58.

To examine a larger root, cut a carrot lengthwise and another carrot across the middle. A carrot is a kind of root called a taproot. A taproot grows downward and sends off smaller roots from its sides. See if you can pick out the smaller roots on the sides of the carrot. Can you see where they come from within the carrot? Look for the tube in the central core of the carrot. Does it extend through the whole root? Other kinds of taproots that we use for food are radishes, beets, and turnips. Can you think of any other roots we eat?

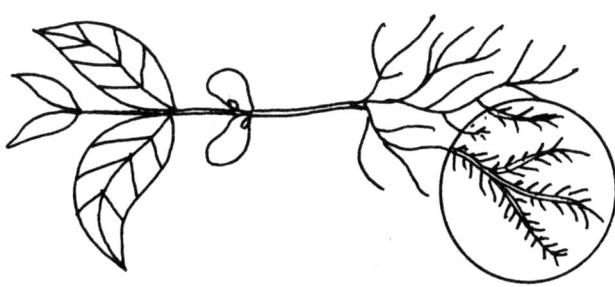

WATER TRAVELS IN STEMS AND LEAVES

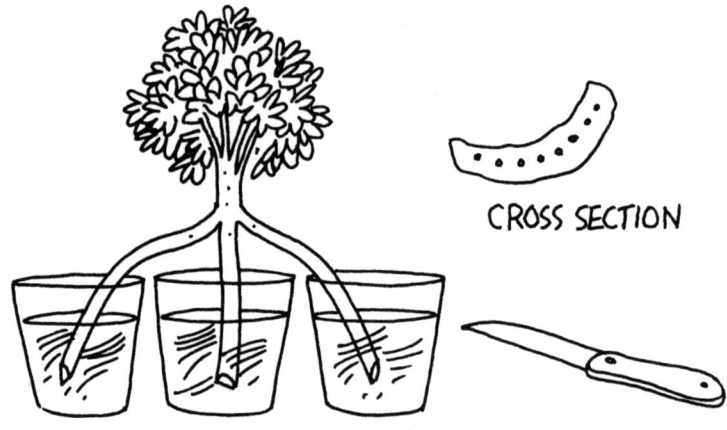

CROSS SECTION

YOU WILL NEED: A stalk of celery with leaves, three glass jars, a knife, water, and ink or food coloring of three different colors such as red, blue, and orange.

WHAT TO DO: Fill the three glass jars with water. Add a different color to each. Add enough color so that the water is strongly tinted. Cut at a slant across the stalk of celery near the bottom. Now make two lengthwise cuts from the bottom to within an inch of where the leaves branch out. You should have three sections of the stalk connected to an uncut section at the top, to which the leaves are attached. Assemble the three jars close to each other and place each section of the stalk in a different jar. Place the jars and the celery in a sunny spot in your room.

WHAT TO LOOK FOR: After a few hours in the sun, observe the colors in the leaves. Does the stalk look colored? Remove the celery from the jars and make a cut across each of the three parts. What are the colored dots along the edge of the cross section? Cut lengthwise along the stalk and try to pull out a colored "string" to see where it goes.

A stalk is one of the stems of a celery plant. The strings are tubes or ducts through which water passes up to the leaves. The leaves of a plant need water and dissolved minerals with which to manufacture food. Other plants have similar ducts in their stems. You can think of the ducts as something like the blood vessels that carry blood through your body.

Notice the pattern of color in the leaves. The colors appear in ducts in the leaves called veins. The colors branch out from a single main vein called a midvein. Each celery leaf has the same kind of vein pattern. Leaves of different plants all have their characteristic patterns. The type of pattern a leaf has is called venation. Look at the leaves of trees such as oak, maple, and birch and try to pick out the type of vein pattern. Look at a leaf of grass and see how its venation is different.

The veins in a leaf connect with the ducts in the stem. Together they carry water and dissolved minerals to all parts of the plant. They also carry the food made in the leaf to the other parts of the plant.

PHOTOPERIODISM

YOU WILL NEED: Four large flower pots, potting soil, a large cardboard box, black tape, and two different kinds of seeds. One kind of seed should be cosmos, dill, or amaranthus, while the other kind of seed should be petunia, dwarf shasta daisy, or dwarf French marigold. These seeds are available in most garden supply stores or from one of the companies listed on page 59. Note: This experiment is best performed during the summer.

WHAT TO DO: Fill the pots with soil. Following the directions on the package, plant about twenty seeds from the first group in each of two of the pots and about twenty seeds from the second group in each of the other two pots. Label each pot with the kind of seed and the planting date. All through the experiment, keep the soil moist but not soggy.

You should get seedlings in about a week. Keep all of the plants on a sunny windowsill in your house. When the young plants are about two inches tall, pull out some of the smaller and larger ones so that you will have about ten average-size plants in each pot.

About four weeks after the plants sprouted, cover one of the pots containing plants of the first group (such as dill) with the cardboard box. Use the black tape to cover all the edges and seams on the box to make sure no light gets through. Cover the pot each day at about five o'clock in the evening and uncover it at about seven or eight o'clock in the morning. Do this every day for a period of two weeks. The other three pots should remain uncovered at all times.

WHAT TO LOOK FOR: Some kinds of plants flower in the spring, some in the summer, and some in the fall. What causes the difference in blooming? Scientists have found that the timing of the

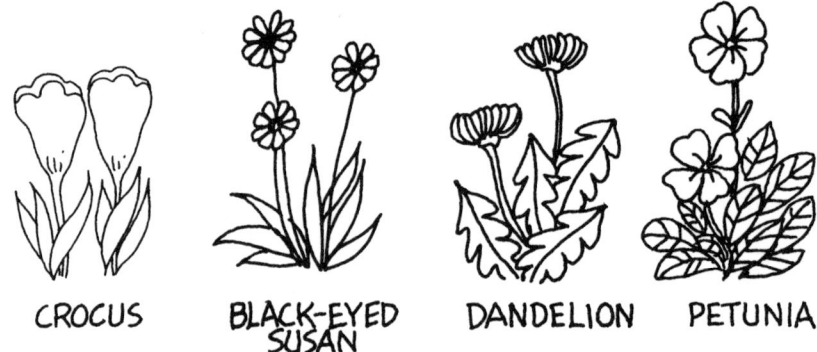

CROCUS   BLACK-EYED SUSAN   DANDELION   PETUNIA

flowers depends upon the length of daylight a plant receives. This relationship is called photoperiodism (from "photo" which means light and "period" which means time).

Some plants, such as the crocus and chrysanthemum, flower when the day length is short. These are called short-day plants. Other plants, such as the daisy and black-eyed susan, flower when the day length is long. These are called long-day plants. Still other kinds of plants, such as the dandelion and geranium, flower whenever they grow large enough. These are called day-neutral plants. The plants in the cosmos group are short-day. The plants in the petunia group are long-day.

Did you affect the blooming time of the short-day plants by covering one of the pots? Did the uncovered short-day plants bloom? How do you know that the covering caused the plants to bloom differently? Try to let the uncovered short-day plants grow for several more weeks. Do these plants bloom when the day-length grows shorter in the fall?

Do the long-day plants from the petunia group flower during the summer? Can you think of any way you can stop them from flowering? Try covering one of the long-day pots with a box so that it receives daylight for a shorter length of time. Does that affect the flowering?

Most plants will not flower under any light conditions until they grow above a certain size and are healthy. In order for these experiments to work, remember to water your plants when needed and keep them in a sunny spot.

SUNLIGHT AND PLANT GROWTH

YOU WILL NEED: Several different varieties of large seeds, such as bean or corn, two flower pots for each kind of seed used, potting soil, and water.

WHAT TO DO: Plant duplicate pots with about five or six seeds of each kind you use. Follow the directions on the seed packet for planting depths: about one-half inch deep is good for bean-size seeds. Label each of the flower pots with the name of the seed; then label one pot of each kind of seed "light" and the other "dark." It does not matter which pots receive either label. Place all the seed-light pots on a windowsill where they will receive sunlight during the day. Place all the seed-dark pots in a dark closet. Keep the soil in all the pots moist but not soggy. The temperature in both dark and light places should be about the same. Keep the plants in these spots until the seeds have germinated and the seedlings are about one week old.

WHAT TO LOOK FOR: Compare the plants kept in a light spot with the same kind of plant kept in a dark spot. Observe the color, size, and number of the leaves on each plant. If the leaves do not grow on some of the plants, they may appear as bumps on the stem. Measure the distance between the leaves or the bumps to see which plants have their leaves more closely spaced. Which set of plants have sturdier stems? Is a taller plant necessarily a healthier one?

According to your observations, do plants grow normally in the dark? What do these plants look like? What makes a plant green (see page 29)? If the plants grown in the dark are not green, what can you conclude?

Large-size seeds, such as beans, contain enough food to allow some growth in the seedling even without sunlight. But what do you think would happen if you kept these plants in a dark place for several weeks? Do you think you could get enough growth for this experiment if you used smaller seeds? Try each of these experiments and see if your predictions were correct.

ARTIFICIAL LIGHT AND PLANT GROWTH

YOU WILL NEED: Two of any kind of household plant such as philodendron, coleus, begonia, or African violet, and a table lamp with a bulb of at least 100 watts.

WHAT TO DO: Place one plant on a sunny windowsill. Place the other plant in a dark corner of the room. Keep the soil of both plants moist. Each day place a lamp one foot away from the plant in the dark corner and allow it to shine on the plant for the same amount of time that the plant on the windowsill receives light. Continue the experiment for at least two weeks.

WHAT TO LOOK FOR: What do you notice about the growth of the plant kept in sunlight compared to the plant kept in artificial light? Compare the size and sturdiness of the stem, as well as the number of leaves and their color. Does the exposure to artificial light produce the same effect as an equal exposure to sunlight?

Does the distance from the lamp bulb affect the growth of the plants? Try the same experiment but this time increase the distance from the bulb to the plant to four feet. Are the results the same as when the bulb was closer? Why do you think this is so?

Does a fluorescent tube have the same effect as an incandescent bulb? Try using a fluorescent light above the plants for several weeks. What results do you obtain? There are several different kinds of fluorescent tubes, including a few that are especially designed for plant lighting. Try out different kinds of bulbs if you can and determine whether one kind produces better plant growth than another kind.

Do all plants show the same need for sunlight? Do some plants grow better in artificial light than others? Try this experiment with several different kinds of plants. Which kinds of plants do you find grow best with the least amount of light? Do some research in books on houseplants to see if your results agree with those of the experts.

LIGHT COLOR AND PLANT GROWTH

YOU WILL NEED: Four small potted plants all of the same kind, four large cardboard boxes, large sheets of blue, red, green, and clear cellophane, and tape.

WHAT TO DO: Cut off the flaps from the top of each box, then cut out one side from each box. Cover the open side of each box with a different color cellophane. Use the tape to keep the cellophane in place. Place one box over each of the plants. Keep the box-enclosed plants in a sunny spot in your room and angled so that the light can enter through the cellophane. Make sure that the soil in each pot is kept moist by watering in the evening when necessary.

WHAT TO LOOK FOR: Are there any differences in the rate of plant growth under the different-colored cellophane? Do any of the plants seem to become sickly? Which of the plants seems to grow best?

Sunlight is not the same color all day long. What color seems to be present in greater amounts during sunrise and sunset? How might you set up an experiment to see whether plants grow as well in the light of morning and evening hours as they do during midday sunlight? What difficulties might you encounter in the experiment?

Some of the cellophane filters allow different amounts of light to pass through as well as different colors. To be sure that the color is the determining factor in different rates of growth, ideally you should adjust each colored cellophane to admit the same amount of light. To do this you would have to use a light meter such as the kind used in photography. Place the meter behind each different colored sheet and point it at the same source of light. Add additional sheets of the same color cellophane to those that have a higher light meter reading until all the readings are the same. You may have to use a dark cellophane of a gray tone to cut down the light received by the plant under the colorless sheet.

Do you think that the kind of plant makes any difference in the color of light needed? Does artificial light make a difference in this experiment? How could you experiment to find out the answers to these questions?

PHOTOSYNTHESIS IN GREEN PLANTS

YOU WILL NEED: A leaf from a green and white coleus plant or from a Tradescantia, alcohol, a double boiler, an electric hot plate, pliers or forceps, and a small amount of tincture of iodine.

WHAT TO DO: Cut off a green and white leaf from the plant after it has been in the sun for a while. Place the leaf in the top of a double boiler and cover it with alcohol. Put the cover on the pan. Place water in the bottom of the boiler and place the double boiler on top of an electric hot plate. Heat the water to boiling for a few minutes. **Caution: Alcohol must never be heated directly because it burns rapidly. For the same reason, keep alcohol away from an open flame. Use the hot plate with care, and turn it off when you have finished with it.** Using the forceps, remove the leaf from the alcohol and place it on a plate. Hold the plate under slowly running water and wash off the leaf. Dilute a few drops of iodine in a teaspoonful of water and use it to cover the leaf. After a minute or two, rinse away the excess iodine.

WHAT TO LOOK FOR: When you boiled the leaf in alcohol, you removed the green coloring matter called chlorophyll. You can see that the alcohol in which the leaf was boiled turned green. The leaf turned completely white or grayish.

You used the iodine to test for the presence of starch. If starch is present, it will turn a blue-black color when you add iodine. Did all or only one part of the leaf turn blue-black? What would you conclude if only the part of the leaf that was originally green turned blue-black?

The process by which starch is produced in green plants is called photosynthesis. ("Photo" means light and "synthesis" means manufacture.) Photosynthesis only takes place in the presence of sunlight in leaves or parts of leaves that contain chlorophyll. Scientists have called photosynthesis the most important chemical reaction on earth. Can you think of why? See page 31 for some clues.

PHOTOSYNTHESIS AND OXYGEN PRODUCTION

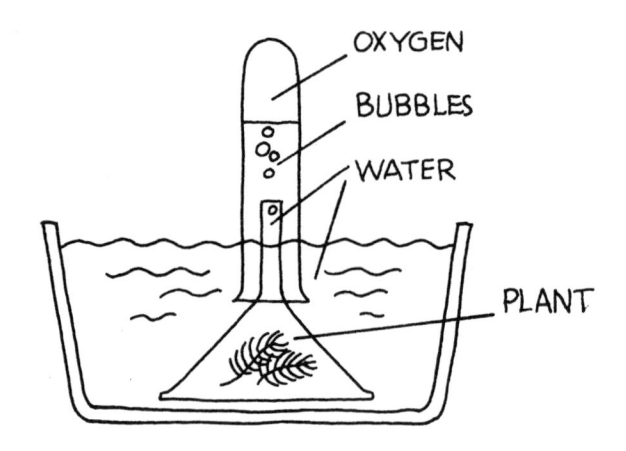

YOU WILL NEED: A water plant such as elodea (can be purchased in a pet store that sells aquarium supplies), two wide-mouthed glass jars, water, two glass funnels, two test tubes, several long wooden splints, and some matches.

WHAT TO DO: Fill each wide-mouthed jar about three-fourths full of water. Place a few sprigs of elodea in each jar and cover the plants with the wide mouth of the funnels. Fill the test tubes with water and place one over each funnel. (See drawing.) Place one of the jars in a bright sunny spot for a day. Place the other jar in a dark closet.

WHAT TO LOOK FOR: Observe the plant kept in the sunlight. You should be able to see tiny bubbles of a gas floating up in the test tube. As the gas rises into the end of the test tube, the water is displaced into the jar. Do you see any gas bubbles rising from the plant kept in the dark? (You'll have to use a light to see.) Does any gas collect in the test tube over that plant?

Test to see what the gas is in the following way. Fill a pan with water. Light a wooden splint and blow it out but leave a glowing spark at the end. Quickly remove the test tube and allow the water to run out. Still holding the test tube upside down, thrust the glowing splint all the way up into it to the top. If oxygen is present, the glowing splint will burst into flame. **Caution: If the splint begins to burn, drop it into the pan of water.**

You have seen in the previous experiment (page 28) that green plants produce food during photosynthesis. But plants produce not only food during this process, but oxygen as well. Oxygen is a gas present in our air. Almost all living things need oxygen. Green plants use carbon dioxide, a gas given off by living things, and water to make starch and oxygen. If plants did not use carbon dioxide, the atmosphere would quickly become unusable for life. Does this help you to answer the question at the end of page 29?

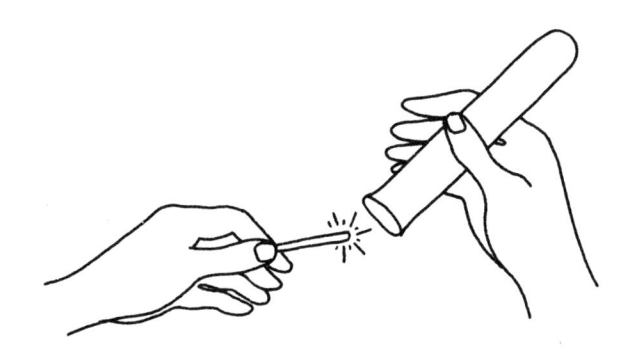

THE GROWTH OF BREAD MOLD

YOU WILL NEED: One slice of fresh bakery bread, paper towel, water, four jars with screw tops, and a piece of moldy bakery bread (see below).

WHAT TO DO: Here's how you can prepare a piece of moldy bread. Use a piece of bakery bread because packaged bread usually contains chemicals to stop the growth of molds. Moisten the bread and leave it exposed to the air on a windowsill for several hours. Then place the bread on a piece of moistened paper towel in a jar. Cover the jar and put it in a warm, dark place for three or four days until the bread turns black.

You can now start your experiment. Cut a piece of fresh bakery bread in four equal-size squares. Take three squares of bread and place each on a moistened paper towel in a jar. Place the other square on a dry paper towel in a jar. Dust a small amount of the mold from the moldy bread on top of each square of bread. Cover the jars and place one moist-towel jar in the refrigerator, one in a sunny spot on a windowsill, the third in a dark, warm spot such as a closet, and the dry-towel jar near it in the same closet.

WHAT TO LOOK FOR: Each day, examine the pieces of bread for signs of mold. Which one grows the fastest? Which the slowest? Do all the slices show signs of mold? Do bread mold plants need moisture? Do they need sunlight to grow? Do they grow better in a warm spot? How do you know?

Why do you think the same kind of bread is used in each dish? For what three different conditions were you testing? Can you think of any other conditions you would like to test to see their effect on the growth of mold?

Molds are a large group of nongreen plants. Without the chlorophyll necessary to make their own food, molds must grow on other kinds of foods. What kinds of molds have you seen? On what kinds of food were they growing? Why does keeping food in the refrigerator help to prevent the growth of molds? How else could you prevent mold growth?

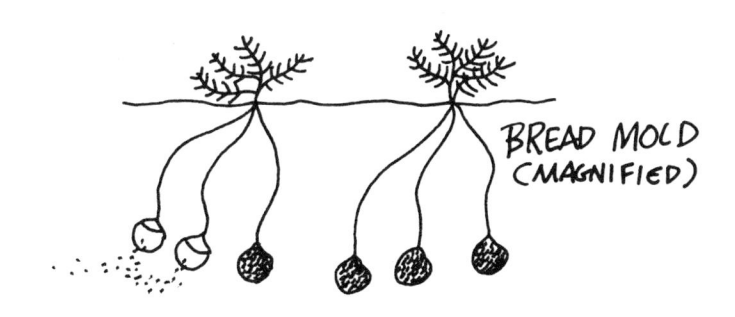

BREAD MOLD (MAGNIFIED)

THE GROWTH OF BACTERIA

YOU WILL NEED: Four empty baby-food jars, aluminum foil, a pressure cooker, an enamel pan, a marking pencil, water, a potato, and the use of the kitchen stove.

WHAT TO DO: Cut the potato into small pieces, and place the pieces along with two cups of water in the enamel pan. Boil the potatoes for about fifteen minutes. After cooling slightly, pour the clear liquid on top into each of the baby-food jars. Fill each about half full. Number the jars 1, 2, 3, and 4 with a marking pencil. Cover each jar with aluminum foil and place all of them in a pressure cooker. Close the cooker. **Caution: Be sure to allow air to escape from the pressure cooker before closing the valve.** Heat at fifteen pounds of pressure for twenty minutes. Allow the jars to cool, then remove them. Let jar number 1 remain covered. Open the cover on jar number 2 and allow it to stay uncovered for half an hour, and then re-cover it. Open jar number 3, touch the contents with your fingers, and then re-cover it. Open jar number 4, lean over it and use your fingers to ruffle your hair over it. Re-cover the jar. Place the covered jars in a dark, warm place in your room. Observe them each day for three days. **Caution: Each time you** handle the jars, wash your hands with soap and water immediately afterwards. Dispose of the jars in the garbage at the end of the experiment.

WHAT TO LOOK FOR: Which jars contain growths of bacteria? Are there the same amounts in each jar? Of course, you cannot see individual bacterium plants. They are too small to see without a microscope. You are looking at large groups of bacteria called bacteria colonies. Do all the colonies in the jars look alike?

Does this experiment help you to see where bacteria are found? Where else besides the places you tested do bacteria live? How do you know? Can you see why it is important to wash up before eating?

Bacteria are nongreen plants, just as are molds, and need food to grow on. Instead of potato broth as food for bacteria, scientists often use a substance called agar. Perhaps you can ask your science teacher to do some experiments with bacteria and agar in school. You might experiment to see the effect of sunlight, cold, heat, and other conditions on the growth of bacteria.

PLANT COMPETITION

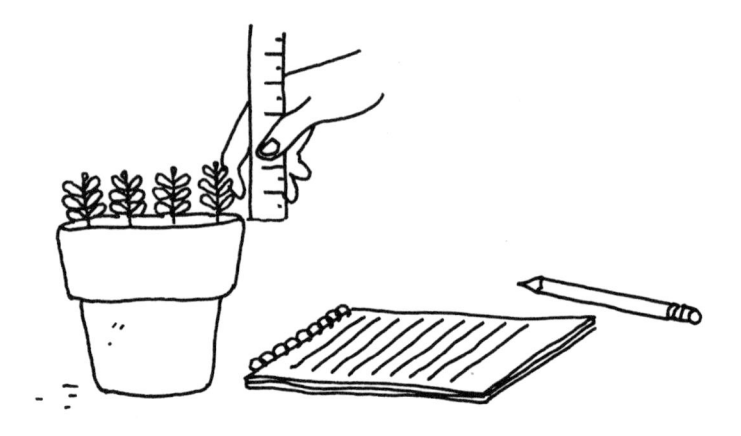

YOU WILL NEED: Four medium-size flower pots, potting soil, water, a package of quick-growing seeds such as marigold, and a ruler.

WHAT TO DO: Fill each of the flower pots with soil. Make small holes about one-half inch deep. In the first pot plant several seeds two inches apart. In the second flower pot, plant the seeds one and one-half inches apart. In the third pot, plant the seeds one inch apart, and in the fourth flower pot plant the seeds only one-half inch apart. Keep the soil moist but not soggy in each pot. Keep the pots in a warm, sunny spot. After the seedlings sprout, pull out any extra plants so that there is only one growing from each hole.

WHAT TO LOOK FOR: Plants compete with nearby plants for available water and nutrients in the soil. They may also compete for sunlight if they grow close enough to shade each other. In nature, weaker plants often die as a result of this competition. But people have learned to space plants far enough apart so that they can grow best.

Observe how the plants grow in each of the flower pots over a period of several weeks. Use a ruler to measure the height of the plants in each pot at the end of each week. Find the average height and compare the growth of all the plants. Which pot grew the tallest plants. Do the tallest plants appear to be the healthiest plants as well?

Compare the number and size of the leaves on the plants in each of the pots. Can you come to any conclusion about which plants grew best? Do you think all plants need to grow at the same distance from each other? Might some kinds of plants be more tolerant of nearby plants?

Would you get the same results if you used fertilizer and added it to the soil in each pot? What effect do you think that might have? Would there be any difference in your results if the plants grew in a shady spot? Perhaps you can try to vary some of the conditions to see what happens. Also try using different-size seeds to see if that influences the distance needed between plants.

PREVENTING PHOTOSYNTHESIS

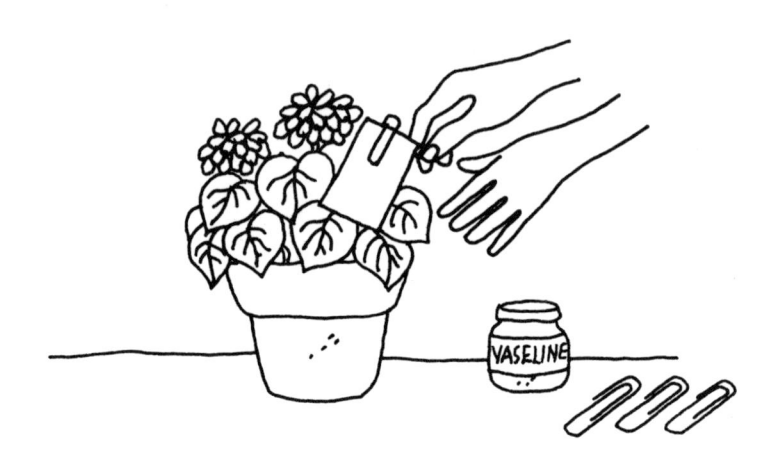

YOU WILL NEED: A potted plant such as geranium or begonia, an index card, vaseline, and a few paper clips.

WHAT TO DO: Use the index card and the paper clips to cover the top of one of the leaves on a plant. Coat the top of another leaf with a thin film of vaseline. Coat the underside of a third leaf with a thin film of vaseline. Water the plant regularly and keep it in a sunny spot for about a week.

WHAT TO LOOK FOR: At the end of the week, remove the index card. Compare the color and appearance of the leaf with the untouched leaves on the plant. What effect does removing light have on the process of photosynthesis? How do you know? You might like to experiment with this leaf to see if it contains chlorophyll (see page 28).

Coating a leaf with vaseline permits light to get to the surface, but prevents carbon dioxide and water vapor from entering and leaving. Was the leaf coated with vaseline on its top surface changed in any way? What happened to the leaf coated with vaseline on its underside?

Perhaps you can explain the difference in results with some additional information. The undersides of leaves usually contain thousands of tiny openings called stomata. You can see stomata with a microscope. See "For Further Reading" on page 58. The topsides usually contain only a few stomata. Stomata can open or close. They allow carbon dioxide to enter the leaf and water vapor to escape. How did the vaseline interfere with this process? What was the result?

GROWING PLANTS WITHOUT SOIL

YOU WILL NEED: Two flower pots, a package of seeds of a fast-growing plant such as radish, a package of vermiculite (available from a garden supply store), a small box of plant fertilizer, and water.

WHAT TO DO: Fill the flower pots with vermiculite. Vermiculite is made from a mineral called mica. It will support the plants and hold water for them but it contains no nutritional chemicals that plants need. If you cannot get vermiculite, try using plain gravel. The disadvantage of using gravel is that you will have to water your plants three or four times each day.

Plant a few of the seeds, according to directions on the package, in each flower pot. Keep their bedding material moist but not soggy. After the seedlings have developed, start to water one of the flower pots with a mixture of water and plant fertilizer. Follow the directions on the package on how to dilute the fertilizer. Continue to water the other pot with plain tap water.

WHAT TO LOOK FOR: After a week or two, you should begin to notice some differences between the plants in each pot. Look to see if there are differences in leaf color, number of leaves, height, and general appearance. What do you think would happen if you continued this experiment for several more weeks?

Most soils contain minerals which are needed by plants. These minerals are dissolved in water and absorbed by plants through their roots. Without these minerals, plants cannot live for very long.

But plants can be grown without soil if you supply the minerals in their water. In fact, plants can be grown just by keeping their roots in a water solution that contains the needed minerals. This method of growing plants is called hydroponics. It is used to grow vegetables and other plants indoors all year long. It is also used in places where the soil may contain dangerous disease germs. In the future, it may be used in a spaceship to grow food for long-journeying astronauts.

PHOTOTROPISM

YOU WILL NEED: Two potted plants such as coleus, a cardboard box, a pair of scissors, black paint, and a brush.

WHAT TO DO: The cardboard box should be large enough to fit over one of the potted plants. Cut out a one-square-inch opening in one side of the box. Use the black paint to coat the inside of the box. The black color will cut down on the reflection of light. After the paint dries, cover one of the plants with the box. Place both plants in a sunny spot near a window. Turn the opening away from the sun. Keep the soil damp in each pot.

WHAT TO LOOK FOR: Remove the box after a week and compare the way the plants are growing. Do the stems and leaves of the two plants seem to be growing in different directions? How can you account for this?

The growth response of a plant as a result of a change in its surroundings is called a tropism. The response of plants in growing toward light is called phototropism. One of the first scientists to study this reaction was the great nineteenth-century biologist, Charles Darwin. Long before he became famous for his theory of evolution, he experimented with growing plants by covering the tips of seedlings or by cutting off the tips. He found that these plants did not grow toward light. But when the plant was completely covered with only the tip showing, it still grew toward light.

Perhaps you would like to try to duplicate some of Darwin's experiments. He worked with a kind of grass called canary grass. You can try using any fast-growing seedlings. Cover the tips of one group of seedlings with little caps made from aluminum foil. Leave another group uncovered. Leave them in the sunlight for several days and observe what happens. After your observations are completed, switch the caps around to the uncovered group and let them stay in the sun for several more days. What happens now? What is your final conclusion?

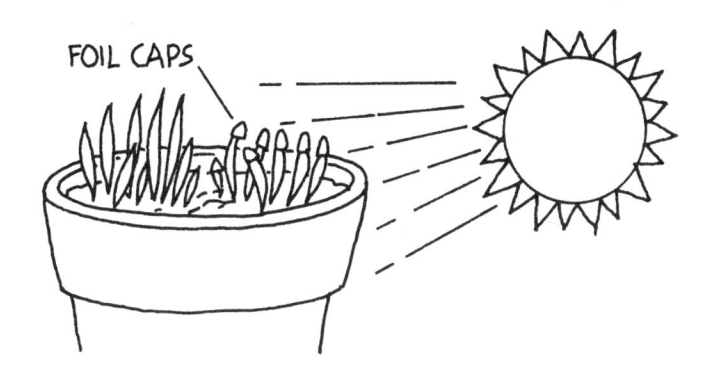

PLANTS IN A MAZE

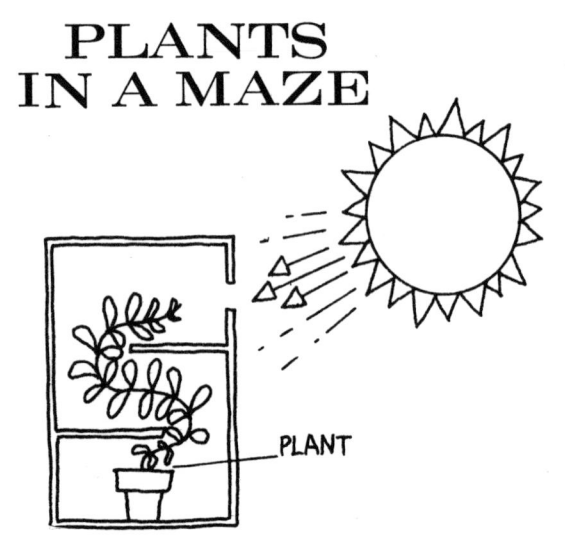

YOU WILL NEED: A shoebox, some cardboard, tape, a small flower pot containing a bean seedling, and a pair of scissors.

WHAT TO DO: Make a maze out of the shoebox by taping two pieces of cardboard in it as shown in the drawing. Cut a small square opening at one end of the box. Place the bean seedling in the box at the other end. Cover the box tightly. Point the opening toward direct sunlight. In the evening you may remove the lid for short periods of time in order to water the plant and observe its growth. Keep the box covered the rest of the time.

WHAT TO LOOK FOR: In what direction does the plant grow? What relation does this experiment have to the previous one? Light reflects around the cardboard baffles and reaches the plant from a different angle in each of the little compartments. This light pattern influences the plant to grow in a different direction in each compartment but always toward the light.

You might be interested in varying this experiment by using more baffles or different plants. Another interesting variation is to cover the opening at the end of the box with a colored sheet of cellophane. Try using the same colors as in the experiment on page 26. (Of course, use only one color at one time.) Does the color of the light have any effect on the growth of the plant?

Can you think of how you can use your knowledge of phototropism to make a vine grow into any shape you desire? Try to devise a maze with many baffles and holes that you can open and shut at different times to train your vine to grow in the shape you want. One indoor vine that is easy to grow is from a sweet potato. Stick some toothpicks into a sweet potato in order to support it and place the bottom of the potato in a jar of water. Keep the potato in a sunny spot until you get some green growth. Then you can use it in the maze.

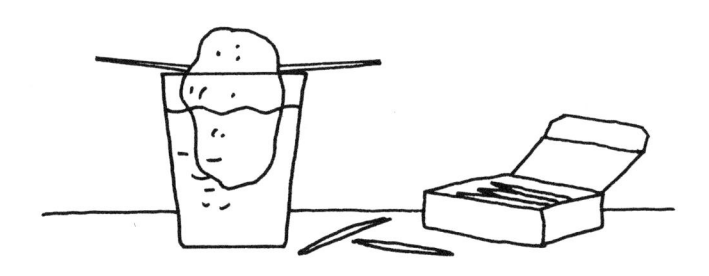

GEOTROPISM

YOU WILL NEED: Two potted plants of the same kind such as coleus or geranium. They should be at least four or five inches tall.

WHAT TO DO: Place both of the plants on a shelf in a dark closet. One plant should be left upright. The other plant should be left on its side in a horizontal position. Observe them each day for a period of three or four days.

WHAT TO LOOK FOR: Plants respond to gravity by changing the direction in which they grow. The change in direction of growth is called geotropism. Growth in the direction of the pull of gravity is called positive geotropism; growth away from the pull of gravity is called negative geotropism.

For what reason were the plants placed in a dark closet? What other factor might have influenced their direction of growth outside the closet? How did the growth of the horizontal plant compare with the growth of the vertical plant? Is this negative or positive geotropism? If the plant left on its side began to curve, at what point on the stem did that happen? The effect of geotropism is greatest where growth occurs.

If you place the curved plant in an upright position, will it straighten out? How long does it take? What do you think would happen if you tried this experiment in a sunny spot in your room? Try it and find out.

How do trees and other plants grow on the side of a hill: at right angles to the sloping ground or at right angles to the horizon? How does this relate to the fact that plants are geotropic?

Roots, as well as stems, are geotropic. But root tips grow toward gravity rather than in the opposite direction. If you remove the soil from a plant left to grow in a horizontal position for several days you can see this effect on the roots. How do the positive geotropism of roots and the negative geotropism of stems help plants to survive?

SEEDS IN MOTION

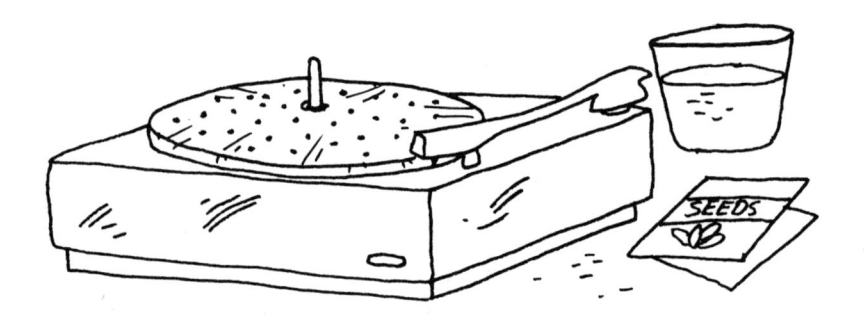

YOU WILL NEED: An inexpensive phonograph turntable, aluminum foil, paper towels, plastic food wrap, water, and a package of mustard or radish seeds.

WHAT TO DO: Cover the turntable of the phonograph with aluminum foil to prevent it from getting wet. Spread the paper towels over the foil, cutting off any parts that extend over the edge. Dampen the towels with water and place the seeds all over the towels one inch apart. Cover the seeds with a sheet of plastic wrap. Start the turntable rotating and keep it going for three days.

WHAT TO LOOK FOR: In what directions do the roots grow from the seeds? Why do you think this is so? Note that water is all around the seeds, so that the roots couldn't just be growing in that peculiar way to get to the water.

If you placed a penny on the edge of a spinning turntable, it would be thrown off. This reaction is caused by centrifugal force. Centrifugal force is the outward pull of a rotating object. Suppose the centrifugal force on a seed rotating on a turntable is greater than the force of gravity. In which direction would the roots grow: toward gravity or toward the centrifugal force?

The tips of roots contain growth chemicals called auxins. Auxins make the plant cells grow faster or slower depending upon their amount and the part of the plant they are in. Gravity usually pulls the auxins downward. But on the rotating turntable, centrifugal force pulls the auxins outward. Can you see how this accounts for the pattern of root growth on the turntable?

Auxins are responsible for all the different tropisms, that is, the responses to stimulation. Some auxins respond to light, others to water, and still others to different stimuli. About fifty years ago, a scientist, Fritz W. Went, was first to isolate the auxin in a living plant. Since that time, hundreds of plant growth chemicals have been found. Some can be bought in plant stores for use with house plants. You can use one of them in the project Plant Growth Chemicals on page 52.

HYDROTROPISM

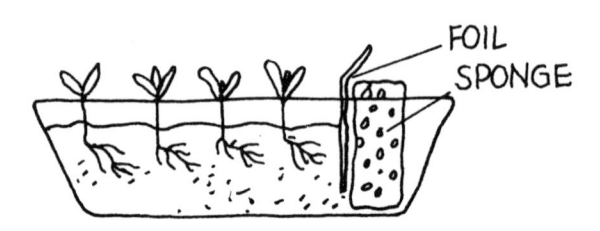

YOU WILL NEED: A clear plastic shoebox or a glass baking dish, potting soil, a flat sponge, water, aluminum foil, and a package of radish, bean, or corn seeds.

WHAT TO DO: Place the sponge upright at one end of the plastic box. Spread a sheet of aluminum foil against it, but leave the bottom inch of the sponge exposed. Fill the rest of the container with loosely packed soil. Plant the container with seeds near the sides so that you will be able to see the root growth. Keep the soil moist until the seeds have sprouted and the seedlings are growing. Then stop watering the soil, but keep the sponge moist. Allow the experiment to continue for a number of days.

WHAT TO LOOK FOR: In which direction do the roots grow? How can you use a dry sponge in another box to set up a control to make sure that the roots are growing toward the sponge because of the water in it? What is the purpose of the control? The growth response of roots toward water is called hydrotropism. Can you explain how hydrotropism helps a plant survive?

An important function of roots is to absorb water through small, fine root hairs. If you examine a root with a magnifying lens, you can see the fuzzy root hairs covering the root. The root hairs provide a larger surface area for water to get into the root. The tiny root hairs easily push their way through the air spaces in the soil. In this way, they are more likely to come into contact with water and the dissolved minerals that plants need.

How do geotropism and hydrotropism combine to make it more likely that a plant root will find water? According to this experiment, which of the two tropisms seems to be more important in determining the direction of root growth? Perhaps you can devise an experiment in which water is in an opposite direction from gravity so that you can see in which direction the roots will grow.

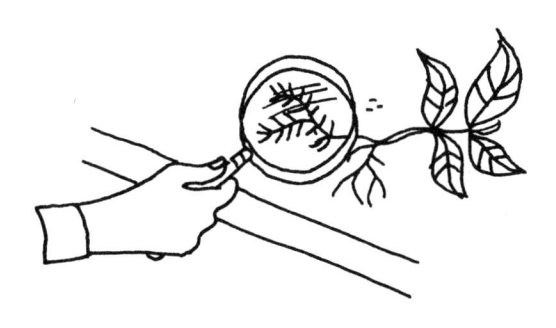

PLANT GROWTH CHEMICALS

YOU WILL NEED: Two potted plants of each type you would like to experiment with (any type of plant will be satisfactory), gibberellic acid (this can be purchased from many plant nurseries or from a scientific supply house), rubbing alcohol, water, and a spray bottle or atomizer.

WHAT TO DO: Prepare a solution of water and gibberellic acid according to the directions on the container. If no directions are given, then dissolve a very tiny pinch of the powder in a few drops of alcohol and add to one-half gallon of water. Use this solution to spray one of each type of plant in your experiment. Spray the entire plant, leaves as well as stem. The unsprayed plant of each type is a control. Make sure that both plants get identical amounts of light and water. Measure the height of each plant daily.

WHAT TO LOOK FOR: Gibberellic acid is a plant growth chemical first discovered by Japanese scientists and later investigated in England and the United States. Several kinds of the acid have been found. Even the smallest trace of a gibberellin was found to make a plant grow large and skinny. Gibberellins almost make true the story of Jack and the Beanstalk. Putting the chemical on a plant makes it shoot up like a beanstalk.

What was the effect of the gibberellic acid spray on the growth of the plants in your experiment? Suppose you used this kind of spray on dwarf plants. Would you be able to produce regular-size plants? If these plants produce seeds, would the seeds grow to be dwarfs or regular size? These are all long-term experiments.

There are many other investigations that you can carry on with plant growth chemicals. For example, do seeds germinate differently when sprayed with a gibberellin? What happens if you add the chemical to only one part of the plant? Does that part grow more quickly than the rest of the plant? Can a plant receive too much gibberellin and die as a result of too rapid growth? What other ideas can you think of to investigate?

MUSICAL PLANTS

YOU WILL NEED: Two potted plants of the same type, a phonograph, and a collection of records that you think your plants might like.

WHAT TO DO: Play your selection of music near one of the plants for several hours each day over a period of weeks. Keep the other plant in a quiet spot. Make sure both plants get identical amounts of light and water. Compare growth and health of the two plants during the experiment.

WHAT TO LOOK FOR: Some people claim that plants grow better if they are talked to nicely or if certain kinds of music are played for them. Other people doubt that this idea can be true.

Some scientists have investigated the response of plants to sounds of different kinds. One definite finding of this research is that plants do respond to ultrasonic sounds, sounds too high-pitched for human ears to hear. Of course, this does not mean that plants "hear" sounds, just that they show various kinds of cellular movement in response to the sound.

Did you notice any differences in the plant that you played music to as compared to the plant that grew in silence? Do you think that these differences might result from the music? How could you continue the experiment to find out if the differences were caused by the music?

Perhaps you can try different kinds of music to see if they have any effect. Try loud music and soft music, classical and popular, western and folk, and any other kinds you can think of. You might also try using different kinds of plants. Perhaps some plants are more musical than others!

Still another experiment that you can try is to talk each day to one plant and not talk to another. Try to build up the plant's confidence. Tell it how well it's growing and how beautiful it looks. Even if you get no results, imagine what fun it will be to tell your friends you've been talking to some plants.

PLANTS THAT EAT ANIMALS

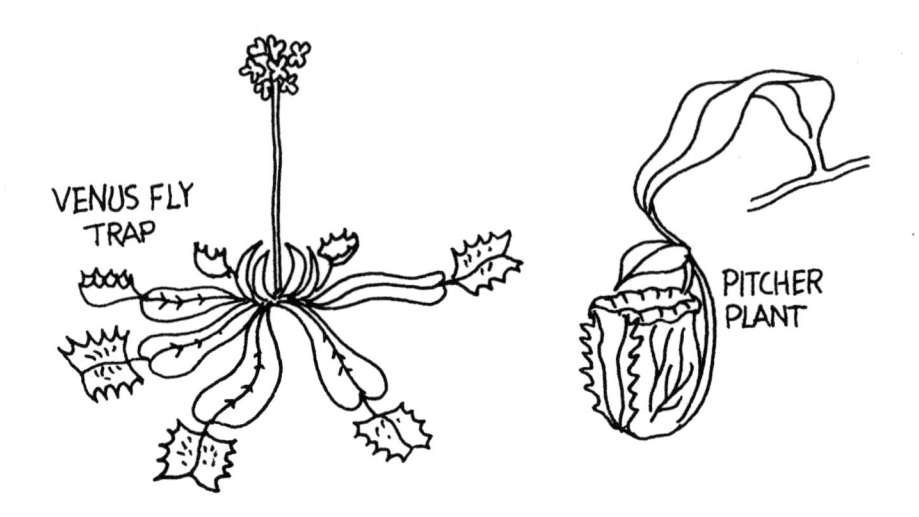

YOU WILL NEED: Any or all of the following plants: Venus fly-traps, pitcher plants, sundews. Also an old aquarium or a large glass container, peat moss or sphagnum moss (available from a garden supply store), and water.

WHAT TO DO: Many local plant nurseries sell Venus fly-trap bulbs as well as other kinds of insect-eating plants. These plants do best in a container that provides warmth, protection against cold air, and a high degree of humidity. Use the moss for planting and be sure to keep it damp. All the plants will root into the moss if you pack it firmly. Don't use fertilizers for these plants. The best kind of water to use is rain or distilled water, but if this is not available, then allow tap water to stand for several days before use.

WHAT TO LOOK FOR: These carnivorous plants all trap insects to supply their needed nutrients, mostly nitrogen. They trap insects in a variety of ways that are all very interesting to watch.

Venus fly-traps have sensitive hairlike triggers on their leaves. When an insect touches these triggers, the leaf snaps together, trapping the insect inside. After a few days the insect is digested and the leaf opens, ready for its next victim. Try touching the triggers on the leaves with the tip of a pencil. What happens? How long does it take the leaf to open when there is nothing inside?

Pitcher plants trap insects in their hollow stems. Downward-growing spines prevent the insect from crawling out. A little pool of water inside the stem digests the insect. How long does this take?

Sundews trap insects on their sticky leaves. The insect can't pull away and is eventually digested. Sundews are found in many places on marshy ground. You might be able to collect some. See the books on page 58 for suggestions on where to look.

Try feeding these plants with a bit of chopped meat. Experiment to see if the leaves will close around other substances such as a bit of wood. Do the leaves stay closed as long around the wood as around the meat? What does that show? What other experiments can you try with insect-eating plants?

VENUS FLY TRAP LEAF

CHOPPED MEAT

FOR FURTHER READING

Bently, Linna, *Plants that Eat Animals,* New York: McGraw-Hill, 1968.

Budlong, Ware T., *Performing Plants,* New York: Simon & Schuster, 1969.

Dickinson, Alice, *The First Book of Plants,* New York: Franklin Watts, 1953.

Hutchins, Ross E., *The Amazing Seeds,* New York: Dodd, Mead, 1965.

Hutchins, Ross E., *This Is a Leaf,* New York: Dodd, Mead, 1962.

Klein, Richard M. & Deana T., *Discovering Plants,* Garden City: Natural History Press, 1968.

Kohn, Bernice, *Our Tiny Servants: Molds and Yeasts,* Englewood Cliffs, N.J.: Prentice-Hall, 1962.

Kurtz, Edwin B. & Chris Allen, *Adventures in Living Plants,* Tucson: U. of Arizona, 1965.

Platt, Rutherford, *This Green World,* New York: Dodd, Mead, 1942.

Poling, James, *Leaves: Their Amazing Lives and Strange Behavior,* New York: Holt, Rinehart and Winston, 1971.

Simon, Seymour, *Exploring With a Microscope,* New York: Random House, 1969.

Simon, Seymour, *Science Projects in Ecology,* New York: Holiday House, 1972.

WHERE TO BUY SUPPLIES

Most of the plants, seeds, soil, and other materials you will need for the projects in this book can be purchased in a plant nursery or garden supply store. For more specialized plant materials you can try writing to one of the following sources. Be sure to ask for exactly what you want.

Carolina Biological Supply Co., Burlington, North Carolina 27215

Turtox-General Biological Inc., 8200 S. Hoyne Ave., Chicago, Illinois 60620

Wards-Natural Science Establishment, Inc., P.O. Box 1712, Rochester, New York 14603

INDEX

Agar, 35
Air:
    needed in germination of seeds, 2-3
    in soil, 51
Amaranthus, a short-day plant, 18-20
Artificial light, 24-25, 27
Autumn-flowering plants, 19-20
Auxins, 49

Bacteria:
    defined, 35
    growth of, 34-35
Beans, seeds of, 3
Beets, 15
Black-eyed susan, a long-day plant, 20
Blooming. *See* Flowering
Bread mold, growth of, 32-33

Carbon dioxide:
    absorption by leaves, 39
    and oxygen, cycle, 31
Carnivorous plants, 56-57
Carrots, 15
Cereal grasses, seeds of, 3
Chlorophyll, 29, 33, 38
Chrysanthemum, a short-day plant, 20
Cold storage of seeds, 9
Competition between plants, 36-37
Corn, seeds of, 3
Cosmos, a short-day plant, 18-20
Cotyledon, 3, 7
Crocus, a short-day plant, 20

Daisy, a long-day plant, 20

Dandelion, a day-neutral plant, 20
Darwin, Charles, 43
Daylight, length of, and flowering, 20-21
Day-neutral plants, 20
Dicotyledon (dicot), 3
Dill, a short-day plant, 18-20
Direction of plant growth:
    auxins as cause of, 49
    in response to gravity (geotropism), 46-47, 49
    of roots, 47, 49, 50-51
    of stems, 46-47
    toward light (phototropism), 42-43, 45, 49
    toward water (hydrotropism), 49, 50-51
Duct system of plants, 17

Embryo, plant, 3

Fall-flowering plants, 19-20
Fall planting of seeds, 9
Fertilizer, 37, 40, 41
Flowering:
    requirements for, 21
    timing of, 19-21
Fluorescent light, 25
Food manufacture in plants:
    chlorophyll and, 29, 33
    lacking in bacteria, 35
    lacking in mold, 33
    light needed for, 7, 29
    minerals needed for, 17
    photosynthesis, 29, 31
    water needed for, 17

Geotropism, 46-47
    auxins and, 49
    and hydrotropism, 51
    offset in turntable experiment, 48-49
Geranium, a day-neutral plant, 20
Germination. *See* Seed germination
Gibberellic acid, 52-53
Gravity, effect on plant growth, 46-47, 49
Green plants, 23
    competition for nutrients, etc., 36-37
    food manufacture in, 7, 17, 29, 31 (*See also* Food manufacture in plants)
    green coloring substance of, 29
    growth of, 7, 22-23 (*See also* Growth of green plants)
    photosynthesis in, 28-29, 31
    sunlight and, 7, 22-25, 36
Growth chemicals, 49, 52-53
Growth of green plants:
    force of, 12-13
    geotropism (against gravity), 46-47
    light needed for, 7, 22-25
    light's color and, 26-27
    phototropism (toward light), 42-45
    tropisms, 43, 49
Growth of nongreen plants:
    bacteria, 34-35
    mold, 32-33

Height of plants, 23, 37, 53
Hillside, plant growth on, 47
Houseplants, light needs of, 24-25

Hydroponics, 41
Hydrotropism, 50-51
    auxins and, 49
    and geotropism, 51

Imbibition, 10-11
Incandescent versus fluorescent light, 25
Insect-eating plants, 56-57

Leaves, 15, 23
    absorption of carbon dioxide by, 39
    chlorophyll in, 29, 38
    escape of water vapor from, 39
    number, size and color, and plant health, 23, 37
    phototropism of, 42-45
    stomata of, 39
    underside versus topside, 39
    veins and vein patterns of, 17
    water needs of, 17
Light (*See also* Daylight; Sunlight):
    color of, and plant growth, 26-27, 45
    conditions, and flowering, 20-21
    plant growth toward (phototropism), 42-45, 49
Long-day plants, 20-21
    plant need for, 7, 22-25

Marigold, a long-day plant, 18-20
Masonry, growth of seedlings through, 13
Meat-eating plants, 56-57
Mineral nutrients:
    absorption by plants, 41, 51
    plant competition for, 36-37
    plants' need for, 17, 41

transportation through plants, 17
Molds:
    defined, 33
    growth of, 32-33
Monocotyledon (monocot), 3
Music, response of plants to, 54-55

Negative geotropism, 46, 47
Nongreen plants:
    bacteria, 34-35
    food manufacture lacking in, 33, 35
    molds, 32-33
Nutrients, plant competition for, 36-37

Osmosis, 15
Oxygen, as product of photosynthesis, 30-31

Petunia, a long-day plant, 18-21
Photoperiodism, 18-21
    defined, 20
Photosynthesis, 28-31
    defined, 29
    oxygen as product of, 30-31
    prevention of, and its results, 38-39
    requirements for, 29
    starch as product of, 29, 31
Phototropism, 42-43, 45
    auxins and, 49
Pipes, underground, damaged by root growth, 13
Pitcher plant, 56, 57
Plant growth chemicals, 49, 52-53
Planting. *See* Seed planting
Positive geotropism, 46, 47
Potting soil, 2. *See also* Soil

Radishes, 15

Roads, growth of seedlings through, 13
Rock, splitting of, by seedlings, 13
Root hairs, 15, 51
Roots:
    auxins (growth chemicals) in, 49
    force of, 13
    function of, 51
    hydrotropic growth of (toward water), 49, 50-51
    as man's food, 15
    mineral intake by, 41, 51
    positive geotropism of, 47, 49
    water intake by, 14-15, 41, 51

Seed(s):
    bicotyledon, 3
    cold storage of, 9
    as man's food, 3
    monocotyledon, 3
    size of, and depth of planting, 7
    structure and parts of, 3
    use of plant growth chemicals on, 53
Seed coat, 3, 11
Seed germination:
    air needs, 2-3
    soil needs, 4-5
    temperature needs, 8-9
    water needs, 2-3, 10-11
Seed planting:
    depth of, 6-7
    in fall, 9
    medium for, 4-5
Seedlings:
    force of growing, 12-13
    light needs of, 7, 22-23
    soil needs of, 4-5
Sewers, damage to, by root growth, 13

Shasta daisy, a long-day plant, 18-20
Short-day plants, 20
Soil, 2
    air spaces in, 51
    mineral content of, 41
    need of seedlings for, 4-5
Soil-less growing of plants, 40-41
Sound, response of plants to, 54-55
Spring-flowering plants, 19-20
Starch production in green plants, 29, 31
Stems, plant, 15, 23
    negative geotropism of, 46-47
    phototropism of, 42-45
    water carrying ducts in, 17
Stomata, 39
Summer-flowering plants, 19-21
Sundew, 56, 57
Sunlight:
    color differences in, at sunrise and sunset, 27
    mold growth independent of, 33
    and photosynthesis, 29, 38
    plant competition for, 36
    plant growth toward (phototropism), 42-45, 49
    plant need for, 7, 22-25
Sweet potato vine, growing, 45

Talking to plants, 54-55
Taproot, 15
Temperature:
    and growth of molds, 33
    and seed germination, 8-9
Tropisms, 43, 49, 51. *See also* Geotropism; Hydrotropism; Phototropism
Turnips, 15

Ultrasonic sound, response of plants to, 55

Venation (vein pattern) of leaves, 17
Venus fly-trap, 56, 57
Vermiculite, 4, 5, 40

Water:
    growing of plants in, 3, 41
    and growth of molds, 33
    imbibition (intake) of, by seeds, 10-11
    intake by roots, 15, 41, 51
    minerals dissolved in, 17, 41, 51
    needed in germination of seeds, 2-3
    needed in plant life, 14, 17
    osmosis of, by root hairs, 15
    plant competition for, 36-37
    root growth toward (hydrotropism), 49, 50-51
    transportation through plants, 16-17
Water plants, 3, 30-31
Water vapor, escape from leaves, 39
Went, Fritz W., 49
Willows, shallow root growth of, 13

ABOUT THE AUTHOR

Seymour Simon is at present teaching science in a New York City school. Mr. Simon is the author of over twenty books, including *Animals in Field and Laboratory, Exploring with a Microscope,* and *Science at Work: Projects in Space Science.*

OUTDOOR EDUCATION LEARNING CENTERS
3830 Richmond Ave.
Houston, Texas 77027